DiscipleWay

7 Disciplines for Maturing in Christ

Worship

Project Directors: Philip Attebery, D.Min., Steve Crawley
Writers: Charley Holmes, D.Min., Donny Hymer, Grover Laird, Mark Livingston, D.Min.
Content Managers: Philip Attebery, D.Min., Chris George, Ronnie Johnson, Ph.D., Jake Vandenburg
Editor: Jerome Cooper
Design Team: Ken Adams, Julie Parker, Larry Thompson

DiscipleWay Worship
ISBN 978-0-89114-476-5

DiscipleWay Worship

Contents

3.0 Introduction 5

3.1 God on God 6

3.2 The Ten Commandments on God 14

3.3 Jesus on God...23

3.4 Worship in Spirit..30

3.5 Worship in Truth...37

3.6 Worship With the Heart 45

3.7 Keep Worshipping From the Heart 58

Key verses for the discipline...65

3.0

Worship

Worship is an incredible topic of study! In fact the topic is too vast to cover all the Bible says about it. The goal of these sessions on worship is to encourage you to increase your knowledge of God and biblical teachings about worship while enhancing your actual worship experience through preparation and Bible-based criteria. Lessons will examine both how and what God has revealed about Himself, what the Ten Commandments indicate as obligations of believers to God, what Jesus Christ taught about the nature of God, what is meant by worship in spirit and truth, and what it means to have a heart of worship.

DiscipleWay seeks to help you learn *how* to perform a discipline (such as worship) by actually performing the discipline together with your fellow disciples. This becomes more complicated with the discipline of worship. Genuine worship demands individuals to prepare for a collective worship experience. These sessions are designed to allow your discipleship team to worship together, to communicate about your worship experience, and to bond as believers through shared worship experiences. Accepting the challenge can bring tremendous reward. The challenge will require faith and a willingness of heart to submit to the Bible's teaching on worship as it applies to both your actions and attitudes as a worshipper.

- The disciple will discover the biblical basis of worship.

- The disciple will be inspired to join with other believers for worship.

- The disciple will prepare for and experience genuine worship.

O come, let us worship and bow down: let us kneel before the LORD our maker. For he is our God; and we are the people of his pasture, and the sheep of his hand.
PSALM 96:6-7

3.1

God on God

Many people have much to say about worship. Ideas range from one extreme to another regarding the nature of genuine worship. Many people have much to say about God. Ideas about the nature of God range from one extreme to another. Because God is to be the sole (only) object of worship, it is important to learn about His nature. Fortunately God has chosen to reveal Himself to His creation most specifically through the Bible.

Lesson Aim: The aim of this lesson is to discover some of what God has revealed about Himself (i.e., God on God). Take a moment to share your understanding about the nature of God and how that nature relates to worship.

> Disciple**Words**
> *Passage: Deuteronomy 4:9-24, 32-35*
> *Key Verse: Deuteronomy 4:10*

Preparation for the trip checklist:
- ✓ I have prayed faithfully for myself and my disciple(s) and/or disciple maker.
- ✓ I have read the lesson aim and text.
- ○ I have read and studied the Bible passage.
- ○ I have memorized the key verse.
- ○ I have arranged for friends and family to participate in worship fellowship.

Direction

Some theologians have said that all theological error begins with a misconception of God. If true, it is of great importance that we understand the nature of God as it relates to worship. This lesson will focus upon God's first public appearance and declarations to the chosen people of Israel. In this passage significant disclosure of God's nature and the intended response of humans are revealed. Take a moment to consider the following question: "Am I prepared to respond appropriately to what I learn about God from this study?"

According to *Connecting With God*, the setting of Deuteronomy is the "end of Israel's exodus from Egypt." The forty years of wandering in the wilderness are now over. Deuteronomy serves to remind the people of why the wandering occurred in the first place (a lack of faith on the part of their fathers, Deuteronomy 1:32-33). It also reminds them of what God had commanded and how He had revealed Himself to them.

Deuteronomy 4:1-8 makes it clear that God expects His people to follow His commands without addition or subtraction (4:1-2). Both evidence of the past and promise of the future declare that careful observance of His commands had resulted in blessing and would result in Israel's great testimony before people of other nations (4:3-8).

Prepare to make observations from Deuteronomy 4:9-24, 32-35.

Observation

1. Who is the author?

2. Who is involved?

3. When was the book written?

4. When does this take place?

A careless or inattentive reading of the passage will likely cause the reader to miss the depth of what is being told. This passage records the first public self-revelation of the nature of God to the people of Israel. The event is originally recorded in Exodus 19 and is retold in Deuteronomy 4. The time between Exodus 19 and Deuteronomy 4 is approximately forty years. God had a purpose in both His message and method of self-revelation. What did God expect the people to learn about His nature? What did God expect in response to His self-revelation? Discover the answers by studying this passage.

5. Are there key words or phrases (nouns, verbs)?

6. Are there words or phrases repeated?

7. Are there comparisons (like, as) or contrasts (but)?

8. Is there a cause/effect relationship (therefore, for)?

historical context?

2. How is the passage affected by its immediate context?

3. How does this passage compare to other related passages?

4. What terms or ideas need to be researched?

9. What form is used (parable, narrative, poetry)?

5. Summarize the passage/paragraph in one sentence (main idea).

Interpretation

1. How is the passage affected by its biblical/

Application

1. Is there a promise to claim or truth to believe?

2. Is there an example to follow?

3. Is there an attitude to change or a sin to confess?

4. Is there a command to obey?

5. Is there a truth to believe?

6. Is there an error to avoid?

7. Is there something to praise God for?

How has the study of this passage increased or altered your understanding of the nature of God? Take a moment to reflect.

Notice that an emphasis is as much on what they did not see as on what they did see.

First, God is emphatic that He did not reveal Himself as anything found in creation (animals, genders, stars, etc.). The only visual description of God is as a cloud, darkness, and fire. Neither of these may be contained. A picture may capture a single moment of a fire. The fire itself is constantly changing. A cloud is the same. While God does not change He is similarly impossible to capture.

Second, God's Word is emphasized. His voice and words (commandments) are clearly intended to be the means of information and inspiration for human response to God. You have studied the value of God's Word from the *DiscipleWay* 1.0 series. The tendency of the Israelites (as recorded in the Bible) was to stray from obeying the commands by using the religious worship practices of the pagan nations surrounding them.

Third, a carved image (i.e., a statue, idol) cannot encompass all that God is. It falls short. The Bible includes the following among God's attributes: immutable/unchanging; omnipotent/all-powerful; omniscient/all-knowing; omnipresent/all-present; holy; just;

love; mercy; true; eternal. The emphasis upon God's not being seen is due to the fact that He is spirit. No one image (animal, gender, etc.) reveals God adequately. It is impossible to create an image of any kind that adequately reflects all the attributes of God.

Worship that is not in spirit and truth leads to error and insufficient views of God. For example a statue of God with strong arms may represent His strength and omnipotence (all-powerful). He is all-powerful, but such a statue might miss the love and compassion of God demonstrated by tender hands or a large heart. A statue may reflect truths about God but any image is insufficient to capture all God is.

Any thought of God not derived from a proper interpretation of the Bible is by nature the product of human imagination. Any concept of God created by human imagination is woefully inadequate. For example some people would say, "My God is love and would never allow someone to...." While it is true that God is love, it is also true that God is just and holy. The Bible clearly teaches that God's eyes are too pure to look at evil and He will not allow the guilty to go unpunished (Exodus 34:7). This is why God chose to reveal Himself specifically through His Word and ultimately through the incarnate (i.e., God in the flesh) Jesus Christ (John 14:6). It should be noted that God also reveals His glory through creation (Psalm 19); however this revealed glory is not intended to reveal the specific grace of God that is available through Jesus Christ.

Fourth, a comparison through all of history and before history demonstrates that the Lord alone is God and there is no other. The revelation of God at Mount Sinai was witnessed by hundreds of thousands of people. Many religions and religious leaders throughout history and modern day have claimed the performance of incredible deeds as evidence of their power and existence. When compared to God's revelation as recorded in the Bible, these fall short of the Lord in every way. The biblical record provides sound evidence of the Lord as the only God, while other religions use stories that are unverifiable and that often qualify as unconfirmed reports.

Could one image or object describe everything about you? Is there a single item, even a visual image (photograph) that explains all that you are? In reality, each human is far too complex to be captured in or by a single image. When one considers how great God is, it becomes evident that no image is capable of explaining Him. He is a "consuming fire." (Deuteronomy 4:24; Hebrews 12:29)

1. What do we do now? This lesson's key verse (4:10) indicates that God intended for

His people to hear His words. The verse also states how God intended for His people to respond to those words. First, they would learn to reverence Him all the days of their lives. Second, they would teach these words to their children and grandchildren. (This may include "close" friends.)

The application for this lesson involves a direct response on your part to God's will in Deuteronomy 4:10. Have you learned to revere Him more as a result of this lesson's study? If so, it is time for you to teach these same things to your children. Here is how. Simply repeat what has been done in this lesson. Use your *DiscipleWay* lesson 3.1 as a guide. Begin with the "Discovery" section and lead through the inductive Bible study questions. This study should help your friends or family to discover truth from God's Word on their own. It is appropriate to repeat ideas learned or used during your original study of the lesson.

2. Carry-Through Activity: What will we do on Sunday?

We will enter the time of worship with reverence for God.

We will recognize that any image of God (real or imagined) is woefully inadequate. (Deuteronomy 4:15-20)

We will pay attention to every presentation of

God's Word during the worship. How will we best accomplish this? (taking notes, etc.)

We will prepare Saturday for worship on Sunday.

How will this be accomplished?(getting plenty of sleep, prayer, Bible reading, etc.)

We will involve our families in preparation for worship on Sunday (i.e., teach them). (Deuteronomy 4:10)

Evaluation

Remember that the aim of this lesson has been to discover some of what God has revealed about Himself (i.e., God on God). Considering what you have learned from the lesson, share your understanding about the nature of God and how that nature relates to worship.

How did you respond to this question from the "Direction" portion of the session. "Am I prepared to respond appropriately to what I learn about God from this study?" Were and are you prepared to respond appropriately to what you have learned?

What went well in your Bible study with your family or friends? What could have been done better?

What have you learned about studying the nature of God and disciple making?

Get ready for the next session

Using the prayer principles you have learned, pray through Psalm 136 and identify the characteristics of God.

Read Romans 1:18-32.

Study Deuteronomy 5:6-15 using the inductive Bible study method.

The Ten Command-ments on God

3.2

Many people are aware that God gave what are known as the Ten Commandments. These commands were given to the Israelites soon after their exodus from bondage in ancient Egypt.

Lesson Aim: The aim of this lesson is to discover what the commands say specifically about a believer's obligations to God and how they relate to worship. Prepare now for the lesson by identifying the first four commandments.

Disciple**Words**
Passage: Deuteronomy 5:6-15
Key Verse: Deuteronomy 5:7

Preparation for the trip checklist:
○ I have prayed faithfully for myself and my disciple(s) and/or disciple maker.
○ I have read the lesson aim and text.
○ I have read and studied the Bible passage.
○ I have memorized the key verse.
○ I have reviewed the previous lesson.
○ I have arranged for friends and family to participate in worship fellowship.
○ I am ready to be evaluated and accountab for my Sunday worship.

Take a few moments to evaluate your recent worship experience by using the "What Will We Do Sunday?" checklist as a guide.

Take a few moments to review lesson 3.1. Remember that Deuteronomy 4:13-14 says that God gave these commandments so they would be followed in the land being entered by the Israelites. Deuteronomy 4:10 places emphasis upon the words of God, reverence for God, and teaching these truths to their children. Lesson 3.1 dealt with God's self-revelation to Israel and emphasized His word. This lesson (3.2) considers the specific words given by God.

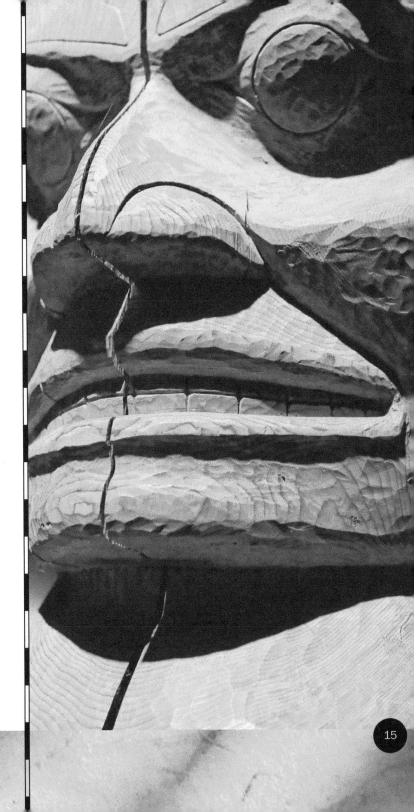

The Ten Commandments may be divided into two main divisions. The first four commands instruct God's people on how to reverence God. The final six commands instruct God's people on how to relate to each other. Jesus recognizes such division in Matthew 22:35-40. He summarizes the entire Old Testament (Law and Prophets) with two commands. The first is to love God with all your heart and with all your soul and mind. The second is to love your neighbor as yourself.

How do you love your neighbor? That is done by keeping the final six commandments (honoring your parents, no killing, no committing adultery, no stealing, no bearing false witness or no coveting possessions of others). How do you love God? That is done most directly by keeping the first four commandments. Because God is God alone, He deserves all we have to offer, including our love, our service, our devotion, and our worship.

Begin discovery of Deuteronomy 5:6-15 by making observation.

Observation

1. Who is the author?

2. Who is involved?

3. When was the book written? When does this take place?

4. Are there key words or phrases (nouns, verbs)?

5. Are there words or phrases repeated?

6. Are there comparisons (like, as) or contrasts (but)?

7. Is there a cause/effect relationship (therefore, for)?

8. What form is used (parable, narrative, poetry)?

Interpretation

1. How is the passage affected by its biblical/historical context?

2. How is the passage affected by its immediate context?

3. How does this passage compare to other related passages?

4. What terms or ideas need to be researched?

5. Summarize the passage/paragraph in one sentence (main idea).

Application

1. Is there a promise to claim or truth to believe?

2. Is there an example to follow?

Pray for clarity for Kyle.

3. Is there an attitude to change or a sin to confess?

4. Is there a command to obey?

5. Is there a truth to believe?

6. Is there an error to avoid?

7. Is there something to praise God for?

First Command — Deuteronomy 5:6 emphasizes the obligation God's people have to obey His commandments. He has delivered them from bondage.

God alone is the proper object of worship. The command teaches that there is only one God. Theologians call this *monotheism*. *Mono* means "one" and *theism* means "belief in God." Having no gods before me literally means that nothing else should be in His presence. Because God is all-knowing and all-present, it is impossible for anything to exist that is equal to Him. How might this command be broken even inadvertently? It is common for some to mix non-Christian beliefs and practices with or during Christian worship. This may be done formally or informally and is a theological error called *syncretism*. It is also common for some to believe that the God of the Bible is simply one of many other gods that exist. This is a theological error called *polytheism,* meaning a belief in multiple (poly) gods. Some actually deny the existence of any god. This is a theological error called *atheism*.

Second Command — It is important to remember the context of Deuteronomy 5:8-10. The Israelites were about to enter a land filled with people who worshipped pagan deities (false gods) primarily through the practices of idolatry. This command is intended to distinguish genuine and acceptable worship of the only true God from the insufficient and corrupt worship of idolatry. Remember the teaching from lesson 3.1 that, "It is impossible to create an image of any kind that adequately reflects all the attributes of God."

It is important to recognize both the truth of consequence and promise of mercy that God declares in this passage. A father's actions affect his children most directly. If a father has chosen to make God His enemy (i.e., hate God) by improper worship, his family, including children and grandchildren, will suffer the consequences. However anyone who chooses to love God and keep His commands will receive mercy from the Lord.

Third Command — Deuteronomy 5:11 regards a person's attitude toward God. A common understanding of this command is that using God's name along with a profane word(s) is what equals a violation. This is true but insufficient. The command goes beyond simple words to the attitude within one's heart. To *take* means "to lift up or carry." The Lord's *name* means all of His attributes and actions! This is more than simply misusing the word (i.e., name) by which He is called. *Vanity* means "to be lightweight, useless, or worthless." For example, when one becomes a follower of Christ he or she *takes* or *lifts up* the name of Christ as an indication that he or she belongs to Christ. His or her negative words and actions demonstrate that the name he/she carries is actually of little value to his or her life. Thus,

to carry the Lord's name properly means to recognize the serious weight of responsibility required of one who claims His name for all of life. In relation to church worship, how do you enter such a service? Do you carry the Lord's name with value or vanity?

Fourth Command — The Ten Commandments are recorded in the Book of Exodus 20 and Deuteronomy 5:11-15. It is interesting to see that the reason God gives for keeping the Sabbath differs in each book.

First, Exodus connects resting on the Sabbath with the understanding (i.e., fact) that God is the Creator. Second, Deuteronomy connects resting on the Sabbath with the understanding that God is the Redeemer (i.e., redeemed the Israelites from Egyptian bondage). God initiated the Sabbath observance as a means of reminding observers that He is Creator and Redeemer. The teaching that God rested after six days of work is best understood as God *ceased* working/creating on the day (i.e., God was not fatigued and in need of relaxation).

It is also true that Jesus Christ is Creator and Redeemer. (John 1:3; Colossians 1:16; Titus 2:14; 1 Peter 1:18-19) The depth of this spiritual truth and its application to believers observing a day of rest is awesome. Christ created and redeemed/purchased eternal life for those who believe. Jesus Christ ceased from His work when resurrected on the first day of the week. Hebrews 4 describes several believers of the Old Testament who did not enter God's rest because of disobedience. Hebrews 4:3 speaks to those who have entered the rest, while 4:11 indicates that believers should make every effort to enter the Lord's rest and avoid following the example of the disobedient ones.

How has this study increased your awareness of your obligations to God in relation to worship?

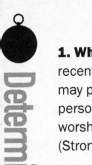

1. What will we do now? Evaluate your/our recent worship experience. This evaluation may provide an opening for discussion of very personal matters regarding each disciple's worship. Evaluate each item using a scale of 1 (Strongly Disagree) to 5 (Strongly Agree).

___ I believe there is one God — the God of the Bible.

___ I have allowed non-Christian influences into my Christian worship.

___ My father(s) chose to hate the Lord.

___ I have chosen to love the Lord regardless of my family background.

___ My words and actions indicate to others that I take the Lord's name (character) responsibly and reverently.

___ I have been faithful in attending worship services.

___ I recognize Christ as my Creator and Redeemer.

What can be done to improve in each area?

Does the teaching found in lesson 3.1 provide help on how you can improve?

2. Carry-Through Activity: What will we do on Sunday?

We will enter the time of worship with reverence for God:

By choosing to love God and worship Him only even if our/my forefathers have chosen to be enemies with (hate) God.

By reflecting upon our/my claims to be a believer and how we/I have carried the Lord's name recently. If necessary, confess the sin of having done so in vain.

By committing to remember the creation and redemption of God and Christ.

We will recognize that any image of God (real or imagined) is woefully inadequate.

We will pay attention to every presentation of God's Word during the time of worship. How will we best accomplish this? (taking notes, etc.)

We will prepare Saturday for worship on Sunday. How will this be accomplished? (getting plenty of sleep, prayer and Bible reading, limiting entertainment to things that edify, etc.)

We will involve our families in preparation for worship on Sunday (i.e., teach them).

Evaluation

What are the first four commands of the Ten Commandments?

How has the study of this passage increased your understanding of the commandments in relation to God and worship?

Get ready for the next session

Read John 17:17 and study John 4:1-42 with the inductive Bible study method. The lesson will focus on John 4:19-24.

Jesus on God

3.3

Much has been written and taught about worship. Many extreme ideas exist regarding the nature of genuine worship. Jesus Christ explained that truth about worshipping God becomes clearer when one understands the very nature of God and the source of truth.

Lesson Aim: The aim of this lesson is to discover the teachings of Jesus Christ regarding the nature of God and resource of truth, thus, what is required for acceptable/genuine worship. Take a moment to share your understanding about the nature of God and how that nature relates to worship.

DiscipleWords

Passage: John 4:1-42
Key Verse: John 4:24

Preparation for the trip checklist:

○ I have prayed faithfully for myself and my disciple(s) and/or disciple maker.
○ I have read the lesson aim and text.
○ I have read and studied the Bible passage.
○ I have memorized the key verse.
○ I have reviewed the previous lessons.
○ I have completed my personal discipleship assignments and am prepared to be evaluated.
○ I have arranged for friends and family to participate in worship fellowship.
○ I have prepared for personal evangelism visitation.

Take a few moments to evaluate your recent worship experience by using the "What Will We Do Sunday?" checklist as a guide.

As stated in lesson 3.1, it has been said by theologians that all theological error begins with a misconception of God. If true, it is of great importance that we understand the nature of God as it relates to worship. This lesson will focus upon two specific attributes of God as explained by Jesus and other biblical passages.

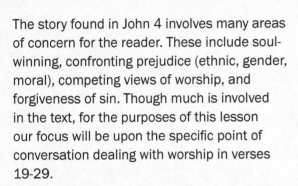

The story found in John 4 involves many areas of concern for the reader. These include soul-winning, confronting prejudice (ethnic, gender, moral), competing views of worship, and forgiveness of sin. Though much is involved in the text, for the purposes of this lesson our focus will be upon the specific point of conversation dealing with worship in verses 19-29.

According to *Connecting With God*, the theme of the Gospel of John is the deity of Jesus Christ (i.e., that He is God). This truth gives Jesus the right to speak with authority on the issue of worship. The land of Palestine was divided into three main regions during the time of Christ. Galilee was the northern region. Judea was the southern region, and the region of Samaria was located between Judea and Galilee. The Samaritan region was inhabited by a mixed bloodline of people from Jewish and Assyrian descent. The Jewish people considered Samaritans as unclean because of their mixed blood. Much prejudice resulted.

Approximately 700 years before Christ, the region of Samaria was part of the Old Testament's "northern kingdom" of Israel that was created after a split from the "southern kingdom" known as Judah.

Observation

1. Who is involved?

2. Where does this take place?

3. When does this take place?

4. Are there key words or phrases in 19-24?

5. Are there words or phrases repeated?

6. Are there comparisons or contrasts?

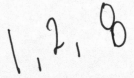

2. How is the passage affected by its immediate context?

7. Is there a cause/effect relationship?

3. How does this passage compare to other related passages?

4. What terms or ideas need to be researched?

Interpretation

1. How is the passage affected by its biblical/ historical context?

5. Summarize the passage in one sentence (main idea).

Application

1. Is there a promise to claim or a truth to believe?

2. Is there an attitude to change or a sin to confess?

3. Is there an example to follow?

4. Is there a command to obey?

5. Is there an error to avoid?

6. Is there something to praise God for?

How does your pre-lesson study of John 17:17 relate to this study?

How does what you learned from your study of Deuteronomy 4 in lesson 3.1 relate to this study?

What word or phrase is common to each passage studied in this 3.0 series?

What has Christ taught about the nature of God?

What are the implications of the nature of God for worship?

1. What will we do now? The encounter between Jesus and the woman at the well is intriguing. Jesus gives an example to His disciples and all believers that demonstrates God's concern for all people is without prejudice toward a person's social, religious, or moral background. The woman is an example of what should happen when a person is actually confronted by Jesus. She was forced to deal with the fact that she was a sinner living in sin. She came to realize that Jesus was and is the Messiah. Her immediate response was to go and tell others simply what Jesus had done and proclaim that He must be the Messiah. It has been said, "It is impossible to come into the presence of God in genuine worship and leave without being changed." While this passage may deal specifically with issues other than worship, it provides a great example of one way a believer may respond to similar encounters with the Lord.

What change should be made in your life as a result of being confronted with the teachings of these passages?

2. Evangelistic Visit. The application steps for this lesson require you to follow the positive examples of both Jesus and the woman. Obedience to the teachings of God's Word and following the example of Christ are acts of worship. Because God is spirit He is not limited to temples or particular locations, He is powerful to work anywhere in the world at any time. Remember from lesson 3.1 that God is omnipresent (everywhere). As Jesus did, make an intentional visit to people you might normally have a temptation to be prejudiced against. Be safe while exercising faith to step away from what is familiar to you. As the woman did, seek to share your testimony and truth about Jesus.

The application steps will allow you to preview *DiscipleWay 5.0*, lessons on witnessing. Forms of prejudice are demonstrated in many ways. In some countries, prejudice is based upon skin colors, social classes, tribes, ages, or genders. Consider visiting a public area (Jesus visited the woman at the well, which was a public area) where you are likely to meet someone different from yourself. Be prayerful. The disciple maker should take the lead and use what he or she has learned from *DiscipleWay 5.0*.

3. Carry-Through Activity: What will we do Sunday?

We will enter the time of worship with reverence for God:

> By remembering what He has done for us/me (specifically His deliverance of me from bondage of sin) and having no other gods before Him. This includes work, material wealth, etc.

> By choosing to love God and worship Him only, even if our/my forefathers have chosen to be enemies with (hate) God.

> By reflecting upon our/my claims to be a believer and how we/I have carried the Lord's name recently. If necessary, confess the sin of having done so in vain.

> By committing to remember the creation and redemption of God and to do good.

We will recognize that any image of God (real or imagined) is woefully inadequate.

We will pay attention to every presentation of God's Word during the time of worship. How will we best accomplish this? (taking notes, etc.)

We will prepare Saturday for worship on Sunday. How will this be accomplished? (getting plenty of sleep, prayer and Bible reading, limiting entertainment to things that edify, etc.)

We will involve our families in preparation for worship on Sunday (i.e., teach them).

We will seek to worship God in spirit and in truth recognizing that He is not limited by time or place.

We will search for a biblical basis for each aspect of Sunday's worship.

Evaluation

What have you learned from this study and what is required for genuine worship?

What have you learned as a result of following the example of Jesus and the woman through the application steps?

Get ready for the next session

Use the inductive Bible study method to study Ephesians 5:15-6:9. Extra attention will be given in lesson 3.4 to Ephesians 5:17-21.

Worship in Spirit

3.4

Destination

Much has been said about being "in the spirit." Jesus makes it clear in John 4:24 that God seeks worshippers who will worship in spirit and in truth. Fortunately the Bible gives both examples and teaching concerning what it means to be in the spirit.

Lesson Aim: The aim of this lesson is to discover what spiritual worship involves and what it means to be filled with the spirit.

Disciple**Words**
Passage: Ephesians 5:15-21
Key Verse: Ephesians 5:19-20

Preparation for the trip checklist:
- ○ I have prayed faithfully for myself and my disciple(s) and/or disciple maker.
- ○ I have read the lesson aim and text.
- ○ I have read and studied the Bible passage.
- ○ I have memorized the key verse.
- ○ I have reviewed the previous lessons.
- ○ I have completed my personal discipleship assignments and am prepared to be evaluated.
- ○ I have arranged for friends and family to participate in worship fellowship.

Review lesson 3.3 and evaluate your recent worship experience by using the "What Will We Do Sunday?" checklist as a guide.

Many opinions exist about what it means to be "in the spirit." Most people, when they hear about spirit, think about certain experiences recorded in Acts. It is important to remember that the book of Acts is a historical record of what occurred in the life of the early church. These events are best understood when interpreted in light of the entire New Testament.

The book of Ephesians is actually an epistle (letter) from the apostle Paul to the church located in the ancient city of Ephesus. Ephesus was a major city in its day and was home to the famous temple of Diana. The nature of worship at this temple often included immoral acts known as fertility rites. These pagan acts of worship were the predominant environment in which the Ephesus church lived and ministered. It is worth noting that these practices of pagan worship were similar to those of pagan worship in the Old Testament.

Read Ephesians 5:15-21.

Observation

1. Who is the author?

2. Who is involved?

3. When was the book written? When does this take place?

4. Are there key words or phrases (nouns, verbs)?

5. Are there words or phrases repeated?

6. Are there comparisons (like, as) or contrasts (but)?

7. Is there a cause/effect relationship (therefore, for)?

8. What form is used (parable, narrative, poetry)?

Interpretation

1. How is the passage affected by its biblical/historical context?

2. How is the passage affected by its immediate context?

3. How does this passage compare to other related passages?

2. Is there an example to follow?

3. Is there an attitude to change or a sin to confess?

4. What terms or ideas need to be researched?

4. Is there a command to obey?

5. Summarize the passage/paragraph in one sentence (main idea).

5. Is there a truth to believe?

6. Is there an error to avoid?

7. Is there something to praise God for?

Application

1. Is there a promise to claim?

How does your study of this passage clarify the meaning of being "filled with the spirit?"

The grammar of Ephesians 5:17-18 in the original Greek language makes it clear that Paul is commanding the Ephesians to stop being unwise and drunk. The grammar in Ephesians 5:19-21 makes it clear that the items discussed there are commands to begin and continue those actions. It is interesting to note the arrangement of the verses that follow Ephesians 5:19. An outline of the passage is obvious. First, speak to one another with "psalms and hymns and spiritual songs." This vocabulary is in contrast to the filthy language described in 5:3-4. Second, sing and make melody in your heart to the Lord. What is the typical music within your heart? Third, give thanks to God the Father for everything in the name of our Lord Jesus Christ. Fourth, is to submit to each other out of fear/reverence for the Lord.

Submitting to each other is further expanded in Ephesians 5:22-6:9. These submissions demonstrate one's being filled with the Spirit. The verses indicate that submission goes beyond being at church to all aspects of life including home and work. Each act of submission is done so in the love of Christ. Those submitting are to be loved by those to whom they submit. Wives submit to loving husbands. Husbands submit to Christ. Children submit to loving parents. Servants submit to earthly masters (bosses) who treat their servants well.

How does this relate to being filled with the Spirit? If a church member does not submit to others in reverence for Christ, he is not filled with the Spirit. If a wife does not submit to her husband, she is not filled with the Spirit. If a husband does not submit to the authority of Christ, he is not filled with the Spirit. If a child is rebellious, he is not filled with the Spirit. If a father is abusive, he is not filled with the Spirit. If a servant/employee does not work hard or obediently, he is not filled with the Spirit. If an employer does not treat his/her employees well, he/she is not filled with the Spirit.

All these must be done in love and by following the loving example of Christ. Each negative action in the preceding paragraph hinders effective worship in spirit. Each positive action in obedience to the teachings of Ephesians 5 and 6 demonstrates one's being in the Spirit and opportunity to worship God in spirit.

1. What will we do now? Evaluate the relationships in your life that are similar to those discussed in Ephesians by rating yourself according to each statement below on a scale of 1 (Strongly Disagree) to 5 (Strongly Agree).

___ I am submissive to members of my church in reverence to Christ.

___ I am submissive to my husband in love.

___ I am submissive to Christ in love.

___ I am submissive to my parents in love.

___ I am a loving parent.

___ I am a good employee.

___ I am a boss who treats my employees well.

___ I use spiritual language when communicating with members of my church.

___ I consistently have a God-honoring song in my heart.

___ I continually give thanks for all the Lord has done.

How would others evaluate you if asked the same questions?

2. Carry-Through Activity: : What will we do on Sunday?

We will enter the time of worship with reverence for God:

> By remembering what He has done for us/me (specifically His deliverance from bondage to sin) and having no other gods before Him. This includes work, material wealth, etc. (Deuteronomy 5).

> By choosing to love God and worship Him only even if our/my forefathers have chosen to be enemies with (hate) God (Deuteronomy 5).

> By reflecting upon our/my claims to be a believer and how we/I have carried the Lord's name recently. If necessary, confess the sin of having done so in vain (Deuteronomy 5).

> By committing to remember the creation and redemption of God and to do good (Deuteronomy 5).

> By submitting to others in Christ (Ephesians 5:21).

We will recognize that any image of God (real or imagined) is woefully inadequate.

We will pay attention to every presentation of God's Word during the time of worship. How will we best accomplish this? (taking notes, etc.)

We will prepare Saturday for worship on Sunday. How will this be accomplished? (getting plenty of sleep, prayer, and Bible reading, limiting entertainment to things that edify, etc.)

We will involve our families in preparation for worship on Sunday (i.e., teach them).

We will seek to worship God in spirit and in truth recognizing that He is not limited by time or place.

We will search for a Biblical basis for each aspect of Sunday's worship.

We will speak to others with spiritual language (Ephesians. 5).

We will sing always with our hearts to the Lord (Ephesians 5).

We will continue to give thanks to God for all things in the name of Christ (Ephesians 5).

We will be submissive in our relationships to demonstrate being filled with the Spirit (Ephesians 5).

Evaluation

Has this study enhanced your understanding of what spiritual worship involves and what it means to be filled with the Spirit?

Has the self-evaluation during the application steps been helpful?

Get ready for the next session

Prepare for lesson 3.5 by doing your own inductive Bible study of 1 Timothy 2:1-15; 3:14-15; 4:9-16. Reading the entire book of 1 Timothy will be helpful to your study. Be sure to read the introductory comments in the "Discovery" section of lesson 3.5 prior to your study.

Worship in Truth

3.5

Many opinions exist as to what is required in genuine worship. What must be present for worship to be genuine and acceptable to God? Jesus Christ made it clear that true worshippers worship God in spirit and truth (lesson 3.2). Fortunately, He identifies the Word of God as truth (John 17:17).

Lesson Aim: The aim of this lesson is to discover what elements of worship are required in the Word of God. Take a moment to share some of what you already know the Bible requires in worship.

> Disciple**Words**
> *Passage: 1 Timothy 2:1-15; 3:14-15; 4:9-16*
> *Key Verse: 1 Timothy 3:14-15*

Preparation for the trip checklist:
- ○ I have prayed faithfully for myself and my disciple(s) and/or disciple maker.
- ○ I have read the lesson aim and text.
- ○ I have read and studied the Bible passage.
- ○ I have memorized the key verse.
- ○ I have reviewed the previous lessons.
- ○ I have completed my personal discipleship assignments and am prepared to be evaluated according to the worship checklist.
- ○ I have arranged for friends and family to participate in worship fellowship.

Direction

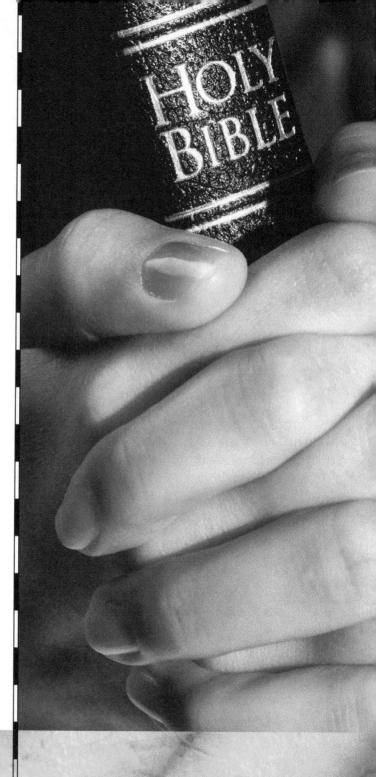

Spend a few minutes evaluating your recent worship experience by using the "What Will We Do Sunday?" worship checklist as a guide.

Spend a few minutes reviewing the previous lesson. The fact that God is spirit allows Him to be worshipped anywhere at anytime. The fact that God is to be worshipped in truth (God's Word is truth) does create boundaries within which worship must occur. In other words, worship must obey the teachings of the Bible. The "Disciple Words" (scripture text) selected for this study give specific instruction for those worshipping God while meeting together in church. These teachings are to be followed by churches until the end of world. You will be encouraged to reference other passages during the application steps.

It is important to remember that the focus of this lesson will be to discover elements of worship that are *commanded* in the Bible. This may contrast with some approaches to Bible study that make historical events of scripture equal to commands. Be careful to ensure that what you consider to be a biblical mandate of *worship* is truly commanded.

Read 1 Timothy 2:1-15; 3:14-15; 4:9-16.

Observation

1. Who is the author?

2. Who is involved?

3. When was the book written?

4. When does this take place?

5. Are there key words or phrases (nouns, verbs)?

6. Are there words or phrases repeated?

7. Are there comparisons (like, as) or contrasts (but)?

8. Is there a cause/effect relationship (therefore, for)?

4. What terms or ideas need to be researched?

5. Summarize the passage/paragraph in one sentence (main idea).

9. What form is used (parable, narrative, poetry)?

Interpretation

1. How is the passage affected by its biblical/historical context?

2. How is the passage affected by its immediate context?

3. How does this passage compare to other related passages?

Application

1. Is there a promise to claim?

2. Is there an example to follow?

3. Is there an attitude to change or a sin to confess?

4. Is there a command to obey?

5. Is there a truth to believe?

6. Is there an error to avoid?

7. Is there something to praise God for?

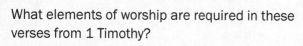
What elements of worship are required in these verses from 1 Timothy?

How do these compare to thoughts shared before the Bible study?

1. What will we do now? The 1 Timothy passage clarifies certain elements that are to be present when the church gathers for worship. Your first objective for this application step is to find biblical command(s) for each element of worship that normally occurs within the context of worship in your church. For example, a pulpit may remind you of preaching. What is a biblical command for preaching within worship? Consider 1 Timothy 4:13; 2 Timothy 4:2. You should feel free to use any scripture that legitimately supports the elements of worship.

The application step will actually involve two segments. First, the disciple maker will arrange for the worship facility (if applicable) to be available for the application step. Be challenged to consider everything that occurs at this location during worship. Consider how people are prepared for worship by how they dress or act as they enter the location. Focus on commandments rather than examples within scripture. Be aware that some items are simply not addressed in the Bible. For example, does the Bible require flower arrangements or a certain order of service? Certain tangible objects may represent elements of worship, but are not essential. Be persistent to find solid Bible basis for each element of worship.

Second, the disciple maker will arrange for a location outside the normal church facility. This assumes that each church gathering is within an actual building. As you know, some churches meet around the world without the benefit of a formal meeting facility. This second segment of the application step, perhaps through imagination, is to visit a location that might be where believers actually would meet in some countries. This might be near a large tree, on a river bank, etc. Explain to the disciples that this location is representative of such a gathering place. Ask them to identify what should occur during a typical worship service in that location. It should become apparent that the same elements of worship in a nice church sanctuary are also required and have the same biblical basis at this location. This should demonstrate that God is spirit and not limited by space or location. Therefore, the truth of God's Word applies to worship at any location and to all believers of all times.

You are invited to pray within the place of worship and thank God for His willingness to reveal His will to His people regarding worship.

Pray that God will help you to worship Him in spirit and in truth and that His Word will always provide the basis for each act or worship within your church. If necessary, ask God to forgive you of mistreating these elements of worship or for not taking them seriously.

2. Carry-Through Activity: What will we do on Sunday?

We will enter the time of worship with reverence for God:

By remembering what He has done for us/me (specifically His deliverance of me from bondage of sin) and having no other gods before Him. This includes work, material wealth, etc. (Deuteronomy 5).

By choosing to love God and worship Him only even if our/my forefathers have chosen to be enemies with (hate) God (Deuteronomy 5).

By reflecting upon our/my claims to be a believer and how we/I have carried the Lord's name recently. If necessary, confess the sin of having done so in vain (Deuteronomy 5).

By committing to remember the creation and redemption of God and to do good (Deuteronomy 5).

By submitting to others in Christ (Ephesians 5:21).

We will recognize that any image of God (real or imagined) is woefully inadequate.

We will pay attention to every presentation of God's Word during the time of worship. How will we best accomplish this? (taking notes, etc.)

Worship in truth of God's Word (1 Timothy 2 and 4) by:

Praying for others.

Praying for authorities knowing that God wants all to be saved.

Praying with holy/clean hands lifted (as a testimony that my bodily actions have been pure).

Dressing modestly for worship.

Supporting the worship in my church that encourages reading of scripture, exhortation and doctrine, use of my pastor's spiritual gifts and meditating upon such things.

We will prepare Saturday for worship on Sunday. How will this be accomplished? (plenty of sleep, prayer and Bible reading, limiting entertainment to things that edify, etc.)

We will involve our families in preparation for worship on Sunday (i.e., teach them).

We will seek to worship God in spirit and in truth recognizing that He is not limited by time or place.

We will search for a biblical basis for each aspect of Sunday's worship.

We will speak to others with spiritual language (Ephesians 5).

We will sing always with our hearts to the Lord (Ephesians 5).

We will continue to give thanks to God for all things in the name of Christ (Ephesians 5).

We will be submissive in our relationships to demonstrate being filled with the spirit (Ephesians 5).

Evaluation

Has your knowledge of what the Bible requires for worship increased? If so, please explain.

Is worship at your church obeying all the Bible commands? It seems that many churches neglect 1 Timothy's command to pray for leaders and all in authority.

The goal of *DiscipleWay* is to enhance the ministry of your church and pastor by emphasizing the need for biblical worship. If appropriate, consider the following questions: What elements are necessary for worship but missing? What things are present but unnecessary?

What role does faith play in worship? Historically, people have attempted to alter worship to meet their own needs or desires. Ancient Israel was notorious for adapting its worship to the surrounding cultures. Faith is essential in worship. Fidelity to the things God commands are not always considered effective

means to reach people for Christ; however, each element must be exercised in faith knowing that God requires obedience rather than human attempts to improve worship.

Get ready for the next session

Bring your children or friends early to the next worship service and share with them the Bible basis for elements of worship. This will be an abbreviated repeat of what you learned in the application steps.

Prepare for lesson 3.6 by doing an inductive Bible study on each of the following passages before you meet for the next lesson: Matthew 15:1-20; Genesis 4:1-6; Leviticus 8-10:3; 1 Corinthians 11:17-34; and Colossians 2:6-23.

Worship With the Heart

The Bible has much to say about worship. It includes both instructions and examples of what God considers to be acceptable/proper acts of worship.

Lesson Aim: The aim of this lesson is to help you discover requirements of acceptable worship as taught and illustrated by selected Bible passages. Once these elements are discovered, an accurate understanding (i.e., definition) of God's ideas for worship should become more clear.

Disciple**Words**
Passage: Matthew 15:1-20
Key Verse: Matthew 15:8-9

Preparation for the trip checklist:
- ◯ I have prayed faithfully for myself and my disciple(s) and/or disciple maker.
- ◯ I have read the lesson aim and text.
- ◯ I have read and studied the Bible passage.
- ◯ I have memorized the key verse.
- ◯ I have reviewed the previous lessons.
- ◯ I have completed my personal discipleship assignments and am prepared to be evaluated according to the worship checklist.
- ◯ I have arranged for friends and family to participate in worship fellowship.

Spend a few minutes evaluating your recent worship experience by using the "What Will We Do Sunday?" worship checklist.

There are many views and opinions used to define worship. The truth is that because God is so vast and superior to humankind, it may be impossible for any one definition to cover all that is necessary to understand genuine worship. This lesson will focus on what selected passages of the Bible say about worship. Take a moment before you study this lesson to share your understanding of genuine worship based upon what you know.

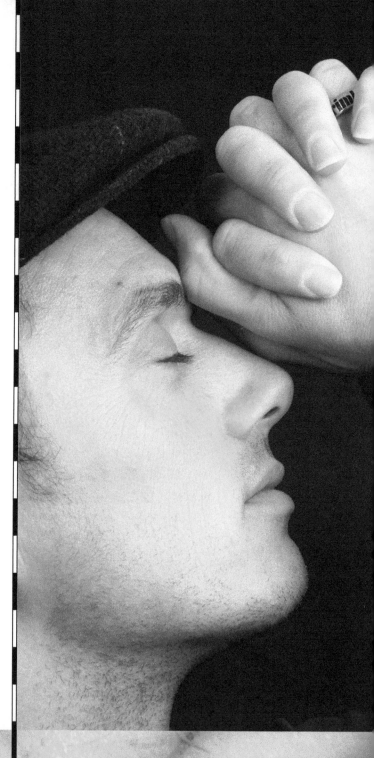

Remember that God is the same in both the Old and New Testaments. Teaching and examples of worship (acceptable and unacceptable) occur in the Old Testament before the establishment of God's laws with His people Israel and during the initiation of His laws with Israel. The New Testament records worship during the life of Christ in the Gospels, and during the life of the early church in epistles/letters. The selected passage for this study is from Matthew 15. The selected passages of your pre-study are from Genesis, Leviticus, 1 Corinthians, and Colossians.

According to *Connecting With God*, the theme of Genesis is "the beginning of the earth, the human race...." Genesis 4 contains the first biblical account of sacrifices made by humans. Leviticus records God's description of the work of the priests. The theme of the book is, "forgiveness through the blood of a sacrifice." These sacrifices were a shadow of Jesus Christ the perfect sacrifice (Hebrews 10:1-14).

Matthew 15 begins with Jewish religious leaders (Pharisees and teachers) asking accusing questions to Jesus. "Traditions of the elders" were regulations that had been added by human interpreters to the Bible's God-given commandments. "Traditions" mentioned in this passage include a special washing of hands and the use of *Corban.* Corban allowed a person to avoid caring for his or her aged parents by apparently devoting his resources to God instead of to parental care. Jesus saw through the appearance of devotion to what it really was, a way for people to keep from obeying the Lord's commandment to honor father and mother.

Paul wrote 1 Corinthians as a letter to a real church needing direction on how to conduct itself during times of worship. Paul also wrote a letter to the church in Colosse while he was in a prison cell in Rome. According to *Connecting With God*, Paul may have never visited the church personally, but he knew people in Colosse and was deeply concerned about false teachings there.

Read Matthew 15:1-20.

Observation

1. Who is involved?

2. Are there key words or phrases?

3. Are there words or phrases repeated?

4. Are there comparisons or contrasts?

5. Is there a cause/effect relationship?

6. What other observation questions should be considered with this passage?

Interpretation

1. How is the passage affected by its context?

2. How does this passage compare to other related passages?

3. What terms or ideas need to be researched?

Application

1. What does the passage say about acceptable worship?

2. Is there a sin to confess, promise to claim, etc.?

Read Genesis 4:1-6.

Observation

1. Who is involved?

2. Are there key words or phrases?

3. Are there words or phrases repeated?

4. Are there comparisons or contrasts?

5. Is there a cause/effect relationship?

Interpretation

1. How is the passage affected by its context?

2. How does this passage compare to other related passages?

3. What terms or ideas need to be researched?

Application

1. What does the passage say about acceptable worship?

2. Is there a sin to confess, promise to claim, etc.?

Read Leviticus 8-10:3

Observation

1. Who is involved?

2. Are there key words or phrases?

3. Are there words or phrases repeated?

4. Are there comparisons or contrasts?

5. Is there a cause/effect relationship?

Interpretation

1. How is the passage affected by its context?

2. How does this passage compare to other related passages?

3. What terms or ideas need to be researched?

Application

1. What does the passage say about acceptable worship?

2. Is there a sin to confess, promise to claim, etc.?

Read 1 Corinthians 11:17-34

Observation

1. Who is involved?

2. Are there key words or phrases?

3. Are there words or phrases repeated?

4. Are there comparisons or contrasts?

5. Is there a cause/effect relationship?

Interpretation

1. How is the passage affected by its context?

2. How does this passage compare to other related passages?

3. What terms or ideas need to be researched?

2. Are there key words or phrases?

Application

1. What does the passage say about acceptable worship?

3. Are there words or phrases repeated?

4. Are there comparisons or contrasts?

5. Is there a cause/effect relationship?

2. Is there a sin to confess, promise to claim, etc.?

Read Colossians 2:6-23.

Observation

1. Who is involved?

Interpretation

1. How is the passage affected by its context?

2. How does this passage compare to other related passages?

3. What terms or ideas need to be researched?

Application

1. What does the passage say about acceptable worship?

2. What elements of acceptable worship have been discovered by searching these selected Bible passages?

1. What will we do now? Prepare for a time of prayer and self-evaluation. The "Disciple Words" from Matthew 15:8-9 should remind all believers of the need to worship God with the heart. Passages such as Psalm 51:10 and 1 John 1:9 remind believers of the need to confess their sins and to seek God's creation of clean hearts within them. Prayer will be guided by the selected passages studied in this lesson. Remember that worship requires discipline. A person who is well-disciplined is able to commit to helpful actions and thoughts while being equally committed to avoiding unhelpful thoughts and actions. Consider how the central principles of each passage describe the disciplined or non-disciplined areas of your own life and heart toward acceptable worship.

2. Pray Through Scripture. Pray through Genesis 4:1-6. Make the following commitments.

Always offer the first and best of what you have in worship (4:4).

Always exercise faith (as Abel according to Hebrews 11:4) in worship.

Always do right things that are pleasing and acceptable to the Lord (4:4).

Offer acceptable worship and not risk mastery by sin over your life (4:6).

Pray through Leviticus 8-10:3. Make the following commitments.

You (friends, family, church) will worship as the Lord commands (8-9).

The glory of God will appear to all people through your worship (9:23).

People will respond to God's acceptance of your worship as in 9:24.

You will only offer things commanded in worship and avoid consequences of disobedience (10:1-2).

You will come near to God in a way that sanctifies and glorifies Him (10:3).

Pray through Matthew 15:1-20. Make the following commitments.

You will follow the commandments of God rather than human tradition (15:3).

Your church will do the same.

You will honor your parents (15:4).

You will not be a hypocrite and worship God only with what you say (verses 7-9).

You will have a heart close to God (15:8).

You will listen and understand what Jesus has to say (15:10).

You will have a heart clean of things that would result in defilement (15:11, 18-20).

Pray through 1 Corinthians 11:17-34 that:

There would be no division within your church (11:17-19).

That your church would observe the Lord's Supper properly (11:20-22).

That you would do things commanded (such as Lord's Supper) in a manner that pleases Him.

That you would have wisdom to discern and discipline yourself so to avoid guilt and judgment (15:27-30).

Pray through Colossians 2:6-23 that:

You will walk in Christ (2:6).

You will be built up in the faith with thanksgiving (2:7).

You will not follow philosophies, deceit, traditions of men or rudiments of the world but Christ (2:8).

You will be complete in Him and grateful for His having made you alive over sin (2:9-15).

You will live as though you are dead to the rudiments/basic philosophies of the world (2:16-20).

You will have wisdom to recognize that teachings of men may appear to be wise but actually do nothing to restrain the sensual desires of the flesh.

3. Carry-Through Activity: What will we do on Sunday?

We will enter the time of worship with reverence for God:

By remembering what He has done for us/me (specifically His deliverance of me from bondage of sin) and having no other gods before Him. This includes work, material wealth, etc. (Deuteronomy 5).

By choosing to love God and worship Him only even if our/my forefathers have chosen to be enemies with (hate) God (Deuteronomy 5).

By reflecting upon our/my claims to be a believer and how we/I have carried the Lord's name recently. If necessary, confess the sin of having done so in vain (Deuteronomy 5).

By committing to remember the creation and redemption of God and to do good (Deuteronomy 5).

By submitting to others in Christ (Ephesians 5:21).

By offering my best and by exercising faith (Genesis 4; Hebrews 11).

By paying attention to the condition of my heart and keeping it near to God (Matthew 15).

By observing the church ordinances (such as the Lord's Supper) without division and in a manner that pleases Him (1 Corinthians 11).

We will recognize that any image of God (real or imagined) is woefully inadequate.

We will pay attention to every presentation of God's Word during the time of worship. How will we best accomplish this? (taking notes, etc.)

Worship in truth of God's Word (1 Timothy 2 and 4) by:

Praying for others.

Praying for authorities knowing that God wants all to be saved.

Praying with holy/clean hands lifted (as a testimony that my bodily actions have been pure).

Dressing modestly for worship.

Supporting the worship in my church that encourages reading of scripture, exhortation and doctrine, use of my pastor's spiritual gifts and meditating upon such things.

We will prepare Saturday for worship on Sunday:

By getting plenty of sleep, prayer and Bible reading, limiting entertainment to things that edify, etc.

By disciplining ourselves to avoid guilt and judgment (1 Corinthians 11).

We will involve our families in preparation for worship on Sunday (i.e., teach them) (Deuteronomy 4).

We will seek to worship God in spirit and in truth recognizing that He is not limited by time or place (Matthew 15).

We will search for a biblical basis for each aspect of Sunday's worship.

We will speak to others with spiritual language (Ephesians 5).

We will sing always with our hearts to the Lord (Ephesians 5).

We will continue to give thanks to God for all things in the name of Christ (Ephesians 5).

We will be submissive in our relationships to demonstrate being filled with the Spirit (Ephesians 5).

We will worship as the Lord commands rather than by traditions of men (Matthew 15).

Evaluation

Review what you have learned from this lesson. Has your understanding of genuine worship changed since the beginning of the lesson? If so, how?

Jesus said the first and greatest commandment is to love the Lord with all heart, soul, mind, and strength (Matthew 22). How can you give Him the first and best of your body, soul, mind, and strength?

What role does the exercise of faith play in these passages?

What application needs to be made to your life?

Get ready for the next session

Prepare for lesson 3.7 by reading Genesis 22:1-19; 1 Samuel 15:3, 9, 20, 22; 2 Samuel 24:18-25; Luke 10:38-42; John 12:1-7; 4:14-21; and Matthew 17:1-5. Give attention to simple observation of what is happening in each passage and the attitude of each participant. Lesson 3.7 will focus on doing the *right* things with the *right* attitude.

Keep Worshipping From the Heart

3.7

Destination

Do you remember the introduction to this series on worship? It mentions the tremendous reward available to those who accept the challenge of learning about disciplined worship. As you have learned throughout the study, the Bible has much to say about worship. There is doubtless much more to be learned.

Lesson Aim: The aim of lesson 3.7 is to learn from the selected examples of others in the Bible regarding both the actions and heart of worship.

DiscipleWords

Passage: Genesis 22:1-5; 2 Samuel 24:24; Luke 10:38-42; John 12:1-7; 4:14-21; 1 Samuel 15:3, 9, 20, 22; and Matthew 17:1-5

Key Verse: 2 Samuel 24:24

Preparation for the trip checklist:

○ I have prayed faithfully for myself and m disciple(s) and/or disciple maker.

○ I have read the lesson aim and text.

○ I have read and studied the Bible passage

○ I have memorized the key verse.

○ I have reviewed the previous lessons.

○ I have completed my personal disciplesh assignments and am prepared to be evaluated according to the worship checklist.

○ I have arranged for friends and family to participate in worship fellowship.

Spend a few minutes evaluating your recent worship experience by using the "What Will We Do Sunday?" worship checklist.

The hope of this series has been to encourage your knowledge of God and biblical teachings about worship while enhancing your actual worship experience. Previous lessons in this series on worship have considered both how and what God has revealed about Himself (3.1), what the Ten Commandments indicate as obligations of believers to God (3.2), what Jesus Christ taught about the nature of God (3.3), what is meant by worship in spirit and truth (3.4 and 3.5), and other requirements of acceptable worship, especially worship from the heart (3.6).

Lesson 3.1 began the series with a study of Deuteronomy 4 on God's self-revelation to the Israelites. Deuteronomy 4:2 teaches that God's Word is to be kept exactly and without additions or subtractions from it. The result of even a slight change can cause a complete disobedience of the commands. Diligently keeping the commands ensures that the right actions are performed in worshipping God. The Bible also makes it clear that the right actions must be accompanied by a right attitude (i.e., a right heart) if God is to be pleased. Changes to the commands of God may reflect a heart that is rebellious or stubborn. A sincere heart

without proper actions may reflect some measure of misunderstanding, ignorance, or even laziness. It is important to always remember the proper attitudes required for genuine worship.

Lesson 3.6 emphasized worship from the heart. Lesson 3.7 continues the idea of worshipping from the heart by observing the examples of several Bible characters.

While most *DiscipleWay* lessons have used inductive Bible study to observe, interpret, and apply each passage, this lesson will use observation primarily to discover the hearts of Abraham, Saul, David, Mary, and Peter as they attempted worship.

1. What has your study of Genesis 22:1-19 revealed about proper worship of the heart (attitude and actions)?

4. What has your study of John 12:1-7 and Mark 14:3-9 revealed to you about worshipping with the heart (attitudes and actions)?

2. What has your study of 2 Samuel 24:17-25 revealed about proper worship of the heart (attitude and actions)?

3. What has your study of Luke 10:38-42 revealed to you about worshipping with the heart (attitudes and actions)?

5. What has your study of Matthew 17:1-5 revealed to you about worshipping with

the heart (attitudes and actions)?

6. What has your study of 1 Samuel 15:1-23 (especially verses 3, 9, 20, 22) revealed to you about worshipping with the heart (attitudes and actions)?

As with Abraham, is your heart willing to submit to the Lord's calling for your life even though you do not know or understand every detail? Are you submitting to the Lord's calling in your life that you are certain of? Are you exercising faith in your worship?

As with David, is your heart willing to confess personal sin? Is your heart willing to listen to God's prophet and obey the Lord's commands? Is your heart and are your actions such that your acts of worship actually cost something of you? Remember this passage during your study on the discipline of giving in the 4.0 series.

As did Martha, are you busy doing many good things for Jesus, but failing to choose to listen to Him? Are you, as Mary, facing ridicule and misunderstanding from your own family?

As did Mary, are you prepared to give what is of great value to the Lord? Are you humble and willing to display such humility in the presence of others? How might such an example motivate your public worship on Sunday? Are you, as Mary, facing ridicule and misunderstanding from those who are leaders and supposedly *closest* to the Lord?

Is your heart willing to listen to Jesus and His instructions for worship? As with Peter, is your heart in the right place, but have your actions been the actual work of your own ideas?

Is your heart willing to obey the Lord's commands? While God's requirements for the Israelite military seem to have little to do with worship, the 1 Samuel 15 passage demonstrates that obedience to God is necessary in every situation. Is your heart willing to submit to the commands of God regarding worship or, as with Saul, is your heart full of rebellion and stubbornness that is trying to "improve" upon what God, the object and author of worship, has already declared?

Carry-Through Activity: What will we do on Sunday?

We will enter the time of worship with reverence for God (Deuteronomy 5):

> By remembering what He has done for us/me (specifically His deliverance of me from bondage of sin) and having no other gods before Him. This includes work, material wealth, etc. (Deuteronomy 5).

> By choosing to love God and worship Him only even if our/my forefathers chose to be enemies with (hate) God (Deuteronomy 5).

> By reflecting upon our/my claims to be a believer and how we/I have carried the Lord's name recently. If necessary, confess the sin of having done so in vain (Deuteronomy 5).

> By committing to remember the creation and redemption of God and to do good (Deuteronomy 5).

By submitting to others in Christ (Ephesians 5:21).

By offering my best and by exercising faith (Genesis 4; Hebrews 11).

By paying attention to the condition of my heart and keeping it near to God (Matthew 15).

By observing the church ordinances (such as the Lord's Supper) without division and in a manner that pleases Him (1 Corinthians 11).

By having a submissive heart even before I know what God would have me do in response to His calling (Genesis 22).

We will recognize that any image of God (real or imagined) is woefully inadequate.

We will pay attention to every presentation of God's Word during the time of worship. How will we best accomplish this? (taking notes, etc.)

We will worship in truth of God's Word (1 Timothy 2 and 4) by:

Praying for others.

Praying for authorities knowing that God wants all to be saved.

Praying with holy/clean hands lifted (as a testimony that my bodily actions have been pure).

Dressing modestly for worship.

Supporting the worship in my church that encourages reading of scripture, exhortation and doctrine, use of my pastor's spiritual gifts, and meditating upon such things.

Choosing to "sit at His feet" rather than become distracted (Luke 10).

Choosing to listen to Jesus rather than add our own ideas to worship (Matthew 17).

We will prepare Saturday for worship on Sunday.

By getting plenty of sleep, prayer and Bible reading, limiting entertainment to things that edify, etc.

By disciplining ourselves to avoid guilt and judgment (1 Corinthians 11).

By disciplining ourselves to offer nothing to the Lord that has been without cost to us (2 Samuel 24).

By examining our own hearts and committing them to obey rather than to rebellion or stubbornness (1 Samuel 15).

We will involve our families in preparation for worship on Sunday (i.e., teach them).

We will seek to worship God in spirit and in truth, recognizing that He is not limited by time or place.

We will search for a biblical basis for each aspect of Sunday's worship.

We will speak to others with spiritual language (Ephesians 5).

We will sing always with our hearts to the Lord (Ephesians 5).

We will continue to give thanks to God for all things in the name of Christ (Ephesians 5).

We will be submissive in our relationships to demonstrate being filled with the Spirit (Ephesians 5).

We will worship as the Lord commands rather than by traditions of men (Matthew 15).

Evaluation of Series 3.0

Do you know more about God and more about worship as a result of this study? What has been most meaningful to you?

Has the "What Will We Do Sunday?" worship checklist been a helpful tool in preparing you for obedient and Bible-based worship?

How will the disciplines of Bible study and prayer be used in worship?

How do you anticipate worship being enhanced by your maturing in the disciplines of giving, witnessing, serving, and leading?

Get ready for the next session

The next session will lead you into another discipline in your growth as a disciple. You will begin to study and practice the discipline of giving.

To prepare for the first session in discipline 4.0, read and do an inductive Bible study of Psalm 24:1-2; learn the aims for the discipline on giving; and memorize Acts 20:35, the key verse for the discipline.

Key verse for the discipline

"O come, let us worship and bow down: let us kneel before the Lord our maker. For he is our God; and we are the people of his pasture, and the sheep of his hand" (Psalm 96:6-7).

3.1 Key Verse

"Specially the day that thou stoodest before the LORD thy God in Horeb, when the LORD said unto me, Gather me the people together, and I will make them hear my words, that they may learn to fear me all the days that they shall live upon the earth, and that they may teach their children" (Deuteronomy 4:10).

3.2 Key Verse

"Thou shalt have none other gods before me" (Deuteronomy 5:7).

3.3 Key Verse

"God is a Spirit: and they that worship him must worship him in spirit and in truth" (John 4:24).

3.4 Key Verse

"Speaking to yourselves in psalms and hymns and spiritual songs, singing and making melody in your heart to the Lord; giving thanks always for all things unto God and the Father in the name of our Lord Jesus Christ" (Ephesians 5:19-20).

3.5 Key Verse

"These things write I unto thee, hoping to come unto thee shortly: but if I tarry long, that thou mayest know how thou oughtest to behave thyself in the house of God, which is the church of the living God, the pillar and ground of the truth" (1 Timothy 3:14-15).

3.6 Key Verse

"This people draweth nigh unto me with their mouth, and honoureth me with their lips; but their heart is far from me. But in vain they do worship me, teaching for doctrines the commandments of men" (Matthew 15:8-9).

3.7 Key Verse

"And the king said unto Araunah, Nay; but I will surely buy it of thee at a price: neither will I offer burnt offerings unto the LORD my God of that which doth cost me nothing. So David bought the threshingfloor and the oxen for fifty shekels of silver" (2 Samuel 24:24).

CPSIA information can be obtained
at www.ICGtesting.com
Printed in the USA
BVHW091455130120
568906BV00003B/7/P